SEASONS, TIDES, AND LUNAR PHASES

Tara Haelle

rourkeeducationalmedia.com

Before Reading:

Building Academic Vocabulary and Background Knowledge

Before reading a book, it is important to tap into what your child or students already know about the topic. This will help them develop their vocabulary, increase their reading comprehension, and make connections across the curriculum.

1. Look at the cover of the book. What will this book be about?
2. What do you already know about the topic?
3. Let's study the Table of Contents. What will you learn about in the book's chapters?
4. What would you like to learn about this topic? Do you think you might learn about it from this book? Why or why not?
5. Use a reading journal to write about your knowledge of this topic. Record what you already know about the topic and what you hope to learn about the topic.
6. Read the book.
7. In your reading journal, record what you learned about the topic and your response to the book.
8. After reading the book complete the activities below.

Content Area Vocabulary

Read the list. What do these words mean?

air pressure
atmosphere
condensation
convection
equator
gravity
hemisphere
humidity
meteorology
momentum
precipitation
radiation
satellites
temperature
tides

After Reading:

Comprehension and Extension Activity

After reading the book, work on the following questions with your child or students in order to check their level of reading comprehension and content mastery.

1. What's the difference between climate and weather? (Summarize)
2. What would happen to Earth if gravity didn't exist? (Infer)
3. What causes climate? (Asking questions)
4. How does climate affect the type of clothes you have in your closet? (Text to self connection)
5. How does the moon affect tides? (Asking questions)

Extension Activity

Create a model that shows how the moon is able to pull Earth's oceans. Put a rubber band on a table to represent the oceans. Put one finger in the middle of the rubber band to represent Earth and the ocean's center of gravity. Then place a finger from your other hand along the inside edge of the rubber band to represent the force the moon exerts on the Earth's oceans. Following a straight line, slowly pull the moon finger away from the Earth finger. What happens?

Table of Contents

In this long photo exposure, you can see how the rotation of the Earth makes it appear as though the stars travel in circles around the poles.

The Sun and the Seasons

Stand in one place and look up at the sky. It probably feels like you're not moving at all. In reality, you're zooming along with Earth at 18.5 miles (30 kilometers) per second around the sun. At the same time, the Earth itself is spinning at 1,040 miles (1,674 kilometers) per hour. It's amazing you aren't dizzy! But just as you cannot feel yourself moving at 60 miles (97 kilometers) per hour in the car, you cannot feel the movement of the Earth. **Gravity** keeps you grounded, and your **momentum**, or speed, matches our planet's.

But you still experience the effects of all that movement. It takes 24 hours for the Earth to complete one complete spin, or rotation. It's daylight for those on the side of the Earth facing the sun and night for those on the other side. The Earth's spin gives us day and night, but Earth's year-long journey around the sun gives us the seasons.

The Earth is not perfectly parallel to the sun. The Earth's axis has a slight tilt of 23.5 degrees because the extra land at the North Pole makes the Earth top-heavy. The Northern **Hemisphere** is tilted away from the sun for part of the year and toward the sun for another part. As the tilted Earth travels around the sun, the angle of the sun's rays hitting the planet changes and causes the seasons.

What's a Leap Year?

It takes the Earth a year to revolve around the sun. Each revolution lasts 365.25 days. Every four years, each quarter of a day adds up to a single day. In those leap years, the year has 366 days, with the extra day on February 29.

The North Star and the Southern Cross

As the Earth travels around the sun, its place in the solar system shifts. That changes our view of the stars. Constellations that are out in summer will dip below the horizon in the winter and vice versa. Meanwhile, the rotation of the Earth also changes the placement of the stars in the sky.

But you've probably heard that the North Star, named Polaris, is always in the northern part of the sky. How can that be? The Earth tilts toward Polaris, and the Earth's tilt never changes, so the North Pole always faces the North Star. When we look toward the North Pole, we're always looking toward Polaris.

A similar star signpost is in the south, called the Southern Cross, or Crux. The five stars that make up the Southern Cross guided explorers as they sailed toward Australia and New Zealand in the Southern Hemisphere.

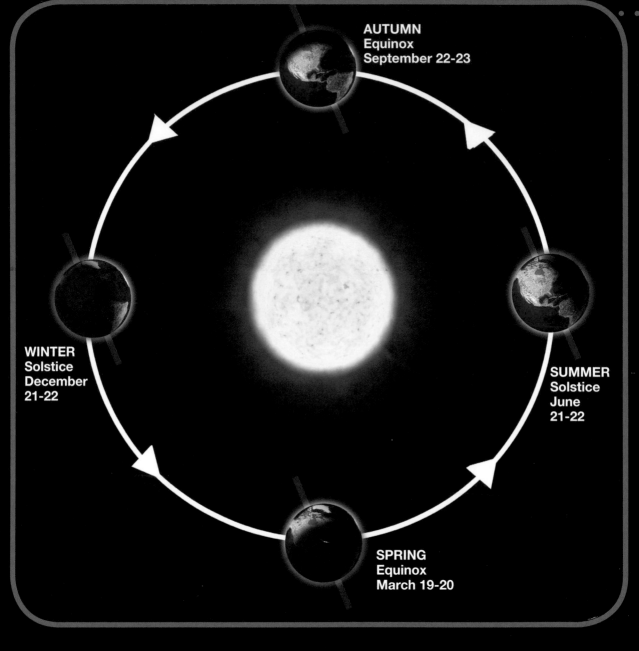

AUTUMN
Equinox
September 22-23

WINTER
Solstice
December
21-22

SUMMER
Solstice
June
21-22

SPRING
Equinox
March 19-20

While the Northern Hemisphere is tilted toward the sun, the sun's rays, called solar **radiation**, hit the Northern Hemisphere more directly. That more direct angle means more heat, giving us summer. At the same time, solar radiation reaches the Southern Hemisphere less directly. The rays travel farther and lose more heat, creating winter in the south. Six months later, when the positions are reversed, the Southern Hemisphere enjoys summer while it's winter in the north.

You might have noticed the days get longer in the summertime and shorter in the wintertime. That's because the sun follows a longer path higher in the sky when it's more directly opposite the Earth in the summer. The longest day of the year is the summer solstice, occurring between June 20 and 22 in the Northern Hemisphere. The winter solstice is the shortest day of the year, when the sun follows the shortest path across the sky. Winter solstice occurs around December 21 to 22. The **equator**, running along the middle of the Earth, gets similar amounts of sunlight all year long because the angle of the sun's rays is similar. Seasons at the equator are also mild.

Spring and Autumnal Equinox Days

Twice a year, the sun shines directly on the equator as it passes from the Northern Hemisphere to the Southern Hemisphere, and then back again. Each of these days is called an equinox. The spring equinox, or vernal equinox, for the Northern Hemisphere occurs around March 19-20 when the sun passes from the south to the north. The autumnal equinox occurs around September 23 when the sun crosses from the north to south. The Northern Hemisphere's spring equinox is the Southern Hemisphere's autumnal equinox.

The farther from the equator you get, the lower the winter sun will sit in the sky because it travels a shorter distance across the sky.

equator

The Moon and the Tides

Just as the Earth revolves around the sun, the moon revolves around the Earth. The moon takes about 27 days to complete one revolution around the Earth. During this time, the moon goes through lunar phases. It appears to get bigger, called waxing, and then smaller, called waning. But the moon really isn't changing at all! It just looks that way. From Earth, we can only see the part of the moon lit up by the sun. How much sunlight reflects off the moon depends on where it is in its trip around Earth.

The Lunar Phases

There are eight lunar phases. The first is a new moon, which actually looks like no moon. A new moon is directly between the Earth and sun and we cannot see the side lit by the sun. As it continues to revolve around Earth, we start to see a small sliver of it, a crescent moon. Next is a quarter moon, when we see a half circle. Halfway between a quarter moon and full moon is a gibbous moon. Finally, we see a completely lit circle, a full moon, halfway through the moon's journey. It passes through another gibbous, quarter, and crescent moon on its way back to a new moon.

Full Moon Craziness

People used to believe that the full moon made people go crazy. The word lunacy, which means insanity, comes from the word lunar. Even today, many people believe the full moon brings more traffic accidents, more crime, busier emergency rooms, and other strange occurrences. In reality, scientists have not found that these things happen any more often during a full moon than at other times during the year.

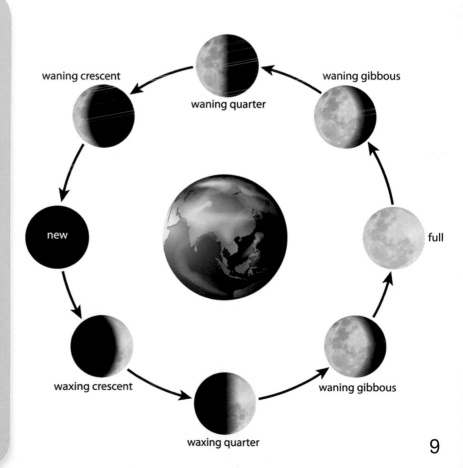

waning crescent

waning quarter

waning gibbous

new

full

waxing crescent

waxing quarter

waning gibbous

Tides

If you've ever been to the beach, you might have noticed the water creep up the beach for part of the day and then fall back. The regular rise and fall of seawater are called **tides**. High tides and low tides each happen twice a day, thanks to a giant tug-of-war between the Earth and moon.

The moon's gravity tries to pull the Earth toward it, but the Earth is bigger, so its gravity is stronger. That keeps us from floating toward the moon. But water is harder to hang onto because it's always moving. The moon's gravity pulls water toward it and creates a high tide on the side of Earth closest to the moon. And on the other side? Those seas also have a high tide. The moon slightly tugs the Earth's core toward it too, pulling the Earth away from water on the other side.

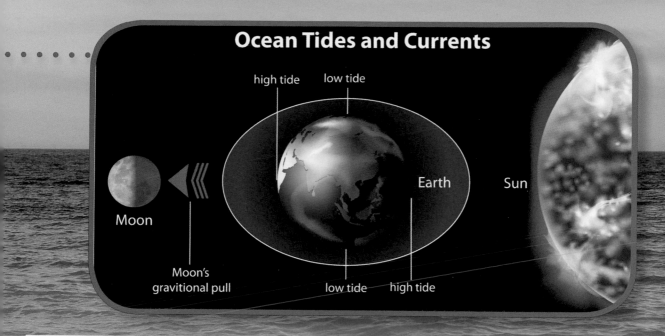

Ocean Tides and Currents

high tide   low tide

Moon

Moon's gravitional pull

low tide   high tide

Earth

Sun

Spring and Neap Tides

About twice a month, exceptionally high tides occur. These are called spring tides and happen during the new moon and the full moon. At these times, the moon is directly aligned with the sun so that the moon, sun, and Earth are in a straight line. The extra gravity from the sun during this time pulls the high tide even higher. The ocean bulge on Earth is an even flatter football.

During the moon's quarter phases, the gravitational pulls of the sun and moon work against each other. The bulge rounds out a bit, and the difference between high and low tide is smaller. These are called neap tides.

You can visualize the tides like a football-shaped bulge around the Earth. Low tides are at the top and bottom of the football, between the high tides. As the Earth rotates, the moon's gravity tows along the world's seas like a giant rotating football.

Where Are the Highest Tides?

The highest tides in the world occur in the Bay of Fundy, between New Brunswick and Nova Scotia in Canada. The difference between high tide and low tide here can be as much as 53 feet (16 meters). That's about as high as five elephants standing on top of one another! The highest tides in the U.S. are in Anchorage, Alaska. The tides can vary by up to 40 feet (12 meters).

Weather Day to Day

Look out the window. Is it raining? Foggy? Sunny? Frosty? The answer, of course, is today's weather. The weather describes how the **atmosphere** acts in a particular area. The atmosphere is a layer of air surrounding the Earth like a blanket. It's made up of gases such as nitrogen, oxygen, carbon dioxide, and water vapor.

The atmosphere is what protects life on Earth from the sun's harsh radiation and the freezing temperatures of outer space. Changes in the atmosphere give us weather.

Many aspects make up the weather: winds, sunshine, clouds, rain, snow, sleet, hail, thunderstorms, and severe weather events. Three key features of weather include **temperature**, **humidity**, and **air pressure**. Temperature refers to how much heat is in the air. Humidity describes how much water vapor is in the air. Air pressure describes the weight of air pressing down on Earth. Interactions between temperature and air pressure drive the weather.

But It Feels Hotter!

Some days, 80 degrees feels like a beautiful 80-degree day. Other days, it may be 80 degrees but feel closer to 90 degrees. What's going on? The humidity is higher on those days when it feels hotter. The heat index is a calculation of temperature and relative humidity that represents what the temperature feels like when you step outside—even if the thermometer reading is lower.

The process starts with the sun's energy hitting Earth. While some energy bounces off, the atmosphere traps most of it. But the sun heats our planet unevenly. Differences in the temperature move air

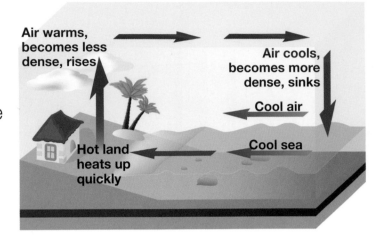

Air warms, becomes less dense, rises

Air cools, becomes more dense, sinks

Cool air

Hot land heats up quickly

Cool sea

around. Heat radiates from Earth and warms the air right above it, causing **convection**. During convection, warm air expands and becomes more buoyant. It then rises and replaces colder air above it. As it rises and spreads out, it cools, and Earth heats the air below it.

Create Wind

You can demonstrate how pressure differences create wind. Blow up a balloon to its intended size, but don't tie it. The compressed air inside the balloon has greater pressure than the air around the balloon. That pressure keeps the balloon inflated. Remember that air with higher pressure moves to areas with lower pressure. Let go of the untied balloon. As the higher pressure air inside it escapes, it creates wind.

These movements cause changes in air pressure. Cold air is denser, so it's heavier and exerts more downward pressure. Warm air is less dense and exerts less air pressure. As warm air rises, it leaves behind low pressure areas. Then air from higher pressure areas swoops in to even out the pressure difference, creating wind.

Coriolis Effect

Believe it or not, wind doesn't move in a straight line. It can't because the Earth's rotation makes it impossible. Since the Earth is wider at the equator than at the poles, the Earth has to rotate faster at its center than at the poles. If you imagine walking down the middle of a giant ball, you would have to walk faster than someone on either side of you who doesn't have to walk as far to keep up with you. The different speed of rotation at different latitudes causes the Coriolis Effect, named for the 19th century French mathematician Gustave Coriolis who first described it. The effect causes air to bend around high and low pressure areas instead of directly into them. In the Northern Hemisphere, wind therefore blows clockwise around higher pressure areas and counter-clockwise around lower pressure areas. The effect is reversed in the Southern Hemisphere.

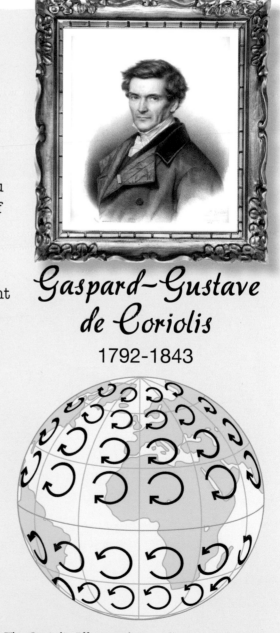

Gaspard-Gustave de Coriolis
1792-1843

The Coriolis Effect explains why tropical storms and hurricanes always rotate around a center.

The Water Cycle

The sun's energy also drives the water cycle, the movement of water through different stages in the atmosphere, on land, and in bodies of water. The water on Earth today is the same water the dinosaurs drank. It just keeps following the same cycle. This cycle, also called the hydrologic cycle, contributes to weather as well.

Most water stays in oceans, lakes, rivers, glaciers, and polar ice caps. Solar energy causes water at the surface to evaporate. Water also escapes from plants through a process called transpiration, similar to the way humans sweat.

Water that gathers on plants as dew results from condensation. But water also evaporates from within plants through tiny pores in leaves called stomata.

During convection when hot air rises and cools, the air becomes denser. Colder air condenses the tiny water vapor droplets into clouds. Through **condensation**, the water changes from a gas back into a liquid, and the water droplets grow larger.

How Fog Forms

Ever dreamed of walking on the clouds? If you've ever walked through fog, you already have! Fog is heavy water vapor suspended in the air, a cloud at ground level. Fog can occur when warm air moves over cold air and pushes it down or when the Earth's surface or a body of water cools off moist air just above it. The fog dissipates as the sun's heat causes the water droplets to evaporate.

Eventually, the droplets become so heavy they fall to Earth as rain, snow, sleet, or hail. This is called **precipitation**. The form depends on air temperature. In freezing air, precipitation falls as snow. If rain passes through a freezing layer of air, it freezes suddenly into sleet. Sometimes, heavy winds in the clouds bounce around frozen crystals until they gather layers of ice, like a snowball gathers snow, and then fall to the Earth as hailstones.

Rain develops when growing cloud droplets become too heavy to remain in the cloud and as a result, fall toward the surface.

Salt of the Earth

The water cycle is also responsible for salt in the ocean. As water hits the ground and flows back to the ocean, it wears down rocks along the way and picks up salt and other minerals from the rocks and soil. The water carries these minerals to the sea. During evaporation, only water vapor rises, leaving the salt and other minerals behind.

The precipitation seeps into the soil or becomes groundwater or runoff, flowing back to the oceans, lakes, and rivers. And the cycle continues.

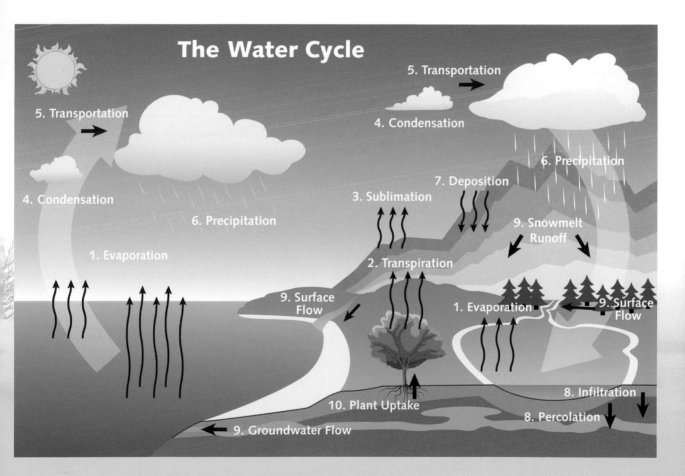

The Water Cycle

5. Transportation
5. Transportation
4. Condensation
4. Condensation
6. Precipitation
6. Precipitation
7. Deposition
3. Sublimation
9. Snowmelt Runoff
1. Evaporation
2. Transpiration
1. Evaporation
9. Surface Flow
9. Surface Flow
8. Infiltration
10. Plant Uptake
8. Percolation
9. Groundwater Flow

Predicting the Weather

Should you go camping this weekend? You'll probably want to check the weather first. Hundreds of years ago, people could only look at the sky and guess what was around the bend. Predicting the weather is still not perfect, but we have many more tools than we used to. The study of weather is **meteorology**. The scientists who track weather conditions and try to predict, or forecast, the weather are called meteorologists.

Most weather conditions in the United States move from west to east, so looking to the weather west of you may offer clues of what's in store. If you live by the sea or mountains, however, the land and water may play a bigger role in your local weather. Meteorologists use a variety of weather instruments to help them gather more precise information to make their predictions.

Relative Humidity

Meteorologists measure relative humidity with a psychrometer, which contains two thermometers, one dry and one kept moist. Relative humidity refers to how much water vapor is in the air at a certain temperature compared to how much water the air could hold at that temperature.

At 90 percent humidity, for example, the air is almost as full as it can be with water vapor. In high temperatures, that relative humidity feels sticky and uncomfortable when you step outside—even if the thermometer reading is lower.

Weather Instruments

One tool meteorologists use is Doppler radar. A large sphere that looks like a huge golf ball sends out radio waves and measures their reflection off precipitation, such as raindrops or hailstones. Meteorologists can then calculate the precipitation's location and speed to make predictions about it.

The United States has 155 Doppler radars, including some in Puerto Rico and Guam. The National Weather Service or the Department of Defense are responsible for most of them.

Some barometers provide sunny and rainy weather icons in addition to pressure readings.

Scientists use barometers to measure air pressure. Barometers either contain mercury that moves according to surrounding air pressure, or they contain a small box that changes shape with changing pressure. Observing air pressure plays the biggest role in weather forecasting because air pressure differences cause most weather conditions. High or rising pressure usually means a nice day. Dropping pressure often means a wet and windy day.

Thermometers measure air temperature. In the U.S., most temperature is measured on the Fahrenheit scale, where water freezes at 32 degrees and boils at 212 degrees. On the Celsius scale used throughout most of the world, water freezes at 0 degrees and boils at 100 degrees.

Anemometers measure wind speed, and wind vanes measure the direction of winds. Rain gauges measure how much liquid precipitation falls, measured in inches or centimeters.

Activity

Make Your Own Anemometer

You can create an instrument to see the speed of the wind.

Materials:

- Five 3-ounce (90 milliliter) paper cups (such as Dixie cups)
- Sharpened pencil with eraser
- Two straws
- Straight pin
- Stapler
- Timer, ruler, marker, and calculator (optional)

Instructions:

1. About an inch below the rim of four cups, punch a hole with the pencil wide enough for the straw to slide through. In the fifth cup, punch a hole in the center of the bottom and four holes at right angles about a quarter inch below the rim.
2. Place a straw through one of the four cups to the other side and staple it to the side of the cup. Push the other side of the straw through two of the fifth cup's holes and then into another of the four cups facing the opposite direction as the first. Staple it to the other cup.
3. Repeat the procedure with the other straw and two remaining cups, setting up your anemometer like the image. All cups should face the same direction, like they're following one another.
4. Place the straight pin through the two straws where they intersect in the center cup. Push the pencil up the middle of the center cup, through the hole in the bottom, until you can press the pin into the eraser.
5. Make sure the anemometer works by blowing into the outer cups to watch it spin. Take it outside on a windy day to see how fast the wind spins the cups.

If you want to calculate the wind in miles per hour, use the marker to put a large X on the top of one of the outer cups. Set the timer for one minute, and count how many times the large X passes closest to you to find out the revolutions per minute (rpm). Then, measure the length of one of the straws in inches.

Do the following calculations with the calculator:

1. Multiply the straw's length in inches x 3.14
2. Divide the answer by 12
3. Divide the answer by 5,280
4. Multiply the answer by rpm
5. Divide the answer by 60

The final answer is the approximate miles per hour of the wind.

Gathering Information

Most U.S. weather information comes from the National Weather Service. This agency uses weather instruments at weather stations throughout the country to learn as much as they can about current conditions. They also send up weather balloons with instruments to measure air temperature, air pressure, wind, and humidity in different areas.

These tools provide many helpful details about weather conditions, but it also helps to look at the big picture. Meteorologists can look at images of the atmosphere from above using **satellites**. Satellites rotate around the Earth taking photos and sending back information.

Weather Balloons

Each weather balloon starts out about five feet (1.5 meters) in diameter, but it expands as it rises to more than 115,000 feet (35,052 meters) above the ground. At about 20 to 25 feet (6 to 7.6 meters) in diameter, it bursts. But during that time as it ascends, it carries with it a small box of weather instruments called a radiosonde. The radiosonde hangs about 80 to 115 feet (24.4 to 35 meters) below the balloon and transmits information on air pressure, temperature, relative humidity, and GPS position every second. The National Weather Service releases about 70,000 radiosondes a year.

Meteorologists combine what they learn from satellite images, weather stations, weather balloons, and radar. Then they

create maps to show where high and low pressure areas are. These maps can show people what temperatures and weather conditions to expect.

25

Severe Weather

A far-off lightning show in the sky can be fun to watch, but severe weather is not so fun to experience. Every year, major storms destroy property, cause injuries, and even claim people's lives. Meteorologists do their best to predict severe weather so people can prepare for a storm, seek shelter, or even evacuate an area.

Storms

Air travels in large masses with similar temperature, pressure, and humidity. Meteorologists track air pressure and moving air masses to predict when a storm is headed your way. When two air masses meet, it creates a front. A warm front occurs when a warm air mass replaces a cold air mass and pushes it down. Warmer, moister air follows it.

When a cold air mass moves into a warm air mass, we get a cold front. The heavier cold air slides underneath the warm air like sliding under warm covers. As the temperature drops and water vapor condenses, rain or other precipitation may fall. Colder, drier air then follows the cold front. Most storms happen during cold fronts, but warm fronts and other air movements can also cause rain.

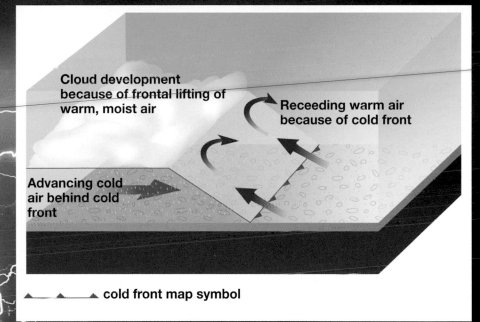

Cloud development because of frontal lifting of warm, moist air

Receeding warm air because of cold front

Advancing cold air behind cold front

▲▲▲ **cold front map symbol**

On a weather forecast map, a cold front is represented by a solid line with blue triangles along the front pointing towards the warmer air and in the direction of movement.

Rainbows

Most rain falls on cloudy days, but rain on a sunny day can bring with it a rainbow. Sunlight shines through raindrops, dividing up the color spectrum like a prism into red, orange, yellow, green, blue, indigo, and violet. But you don't have to wait for rain on a sunny day to see a rainbow. Turn on a sprinkler and stand with your back to the sun. Peering through the mist of the sprinkler will show you a rainbow too.

27

Mosh pits are crowded dance areas at concerts, where people bounce off each other on purpose.

Thunderstorms

Thunderstorms happen when an air mass rapidly rises and forms large, flat-topped clouds. Inside the clouds, powerful air currents push around water droplets and ice crystals. These droplets crash into each other like a giant mosh pit. The friction from these crashing particles builds up static electricity.

The electricity keeps building until it becomes so powerful it has to escape. That's when a giant spark leaps across the cloud or from the cloud to the ground. That giant spark is lightning. The sound it makes is thunder. We see the lightning before we hear the thunder because light travels faster than sound. Lightning can heat the surrounding air to 54,000 degrees Fahrenheit (30,000 degrees Celsius), five times hotter than the sun!

How Far Is the Lightning?

You can estimate how far away lightning is by counting how long it takes for the sound of the thunder to reach you. Sound travels an average of 1,200 feet (365.76 meters) per second, or about one mile (1.6 kilometers) every five seconds. Once you see a bolt, start counting in seconds. When you hear the thunder, divide by five to find out how many miles away it is.

Floods and Blizzards

When rain pounds the Earth faster than the land and bodies of water can absorb it, it causes flooding. Floods can destroy property and endanger people and animals. Flash floods happen suddenly, especially when local rivers or lakes overflow. Floods can also occur when a natural or manmade barrier, such as a dam, breaches or breaks. Strong storms, like hurricanes, can cause flooding by pushing water from an ocean or lake onto the land, in a storm surge.

Hurricane Sandy's storm surge peaked through three high tides, which magnified its effect. To make it worse, it occurred during a full moon when tides are already at their highest level. It was the deadliest and most destructive hurricane of the 2012 Atlantic hurricane season.

City officials expecting a blizzard may call a state of emergency to shut down roads and prevent accidents and stranded drivers.

Just as excessive rains cause floods, excessive snow and high winds cause blizzards. These winter storms can completely shut down a city or a region. In whiteout conditions, it's impossible to see through the heavy snowfall. Another severe winter storm is an ice storm. Rain or sleet freezes on the ground and makes it dangerous to drive or even walk.

It's Raining Fish!

A tornado that forms or moves over water becomes a waterspout, a massive column of water containing whatever it sucked up from a sea or lake. If the waterspout heads to shore, it can rain down fish, crabs, jellyfish, and whatever other sea creatures it picked up during its journey.

31

Tropical Storms and Hurricanes

Hurricanes start as tropical storms over the ocean. Air rises from warm water and creates a small area of extremely low pressure. Higher pressure air rushes in so quickly to fill the gap that winds begin swirling around the center at high speeds. When the winds reach at least 74 miles (119 kilometers) per hour, the storm becomes a hurricane.

The center becomes the eye of the hurricane, the relatively calm lowest pressure area. An eye can measure about 20 to 40 miles (32 to 64 kilometers) across, but the whole hurricane might be several hundred miles across and reach speeds of 185 miles (300 kilometers) per hour. When a hurricane moves over land or cold water, it begins to slow down.

The word hurricane *originates from the Spanish word* huracán, *which came from* hurakán, *meaning "god of the storm" in the indigenous Caribbean language Taíno.*

What's in a Name?

What Americans call hurricanes have a different name elsewhere in the world. Any low-pressure system pulling in rapidly rotating winds is called a cyclone. If the cyclone occurs in the Northern Hemisphere around the Americas, Europe, and Africa, it spins counter-clockwise and is called a hurricane. But near Asia in the Western Pacific, cyclones are called typhoons. In the Southern Hemisphere, they're simply called cyclones, but they spin clockwise.

Hurricane Categories

Meteorologists classify hurricanes based on wind speeds and the damage they cause. The list of five categories is called the Saffir-Simpson wind scale.

CATEGORY	WIND SPEEDS	CAUSES
One	74-95 miles per hour (119-153 km/h)	light damage to buildings, uprooted trees, short-term power outages
Two	96-110 miles per hour (154-177 km/h)	moderate damage to buildings, uprooted trees, severe and long-lasting power outages
Three	111-129 miles per hour (178-208 km/h)	significant damage to buildings, uprooted trees, power and water outages for days or weeks
Four	130-156 miles per hour (209-251 km/h)	severe damage to buildings, with some destroyed, uprooted trees, power outages and unfit for living for weeks or months
Five	157 miles per hour (252 km/h) or higher	extremely severe destruction to buildings with many completely collapsed or destroyed, uprooted trees, power outages and unfit for living for weeks or months

Tornadoes

Meteorologists usually have plenty of warning for a forming hurricane, but not for tornadoes. Tornadoes are much smaller and occur in different areas than hurricanes. They form when a severely low pressure area draws in forceful winds that begin rapidly circling the center, sometimes more than 300 miles (480 kilometers) per hour. The column of swirling air becomes a funnel cloud that violently sweeps across the ground causing destruction.

Tornado Alley

A tornado can form anywhere the conditions are right, but the central, southern plains of the United States see far more tornadoes than most other parts of the world. The nickname for this region is Tornado Alley.

It extends roughly from central Texas north to South Dakota and includes most of Oklahoma, Kansas, and Nebraska. Tornado season in this area runs from about late spring to early fall.

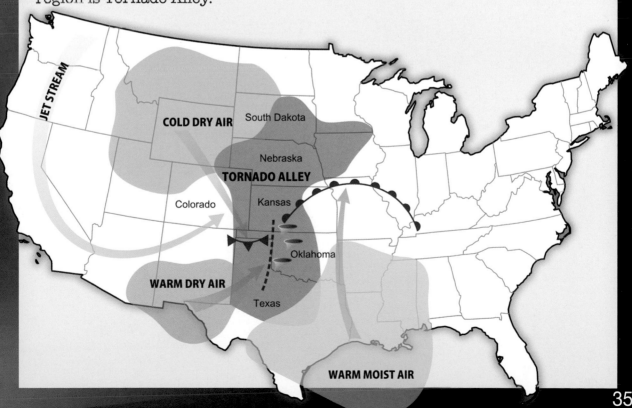

JET STREAM

COLD DRY AIR   South Dakota

Nebraska

TORNADO ALLEY

Colorado   Kansas

WARM DRY AIR

Oklahoma

Texas

WARM MOIST AIR

Climate Across the World

Each day has its own weather, but climate describes long-term weather patterns. The average temperature, precipitation, humidity, wind speed, and storms over at least 30 years make up a region's climate. In some places, cycles of floods or droughts may be a normal part of the local climate. Other places may have climates with few weather changes or temporary variations.

El Niño

Even in regions with stable climates, variations can occur due to sun storms or other events. One such event is El Niño, a weather pattern that brings more rain and higher temperatures. El Niño is Spanish for "little boy" since the weather seems to throw a temper tantrum during El Niño years.

El Niño occurs every few years and starts with warmer than usual water near the equator in the Pacific Ocean. The warm ocean currents carry tropical fish further north, and the Eastern U.S. usually experiences a milder winter than usual.

Climate has a major impact on all creatures on Earth. The weather might affect what you wear today, but climate affects what your wardrobe looks like. People in Florida might own more swimsuits, but Alaskans own more snowsuits.

Climate helps shape mountains, rivers, and the land. It influences the shelters people build and the food they grow to survive. Climate also affects what types of plants and animals live in particular regions and their behaviors, such as hibernation or migration patterns.

The snowy climate of Greenland, Alaska, and northern Canada meant that the Inuit, the native people to these areas, built igloos out of ice and snow for shelter.

37

What Causes Climate?

A region's distance from the equator, called its latitude, plays a big role in its climate. The tropical zones around the equator are usually warmest because they get the most energy from the sun. The polar regions farthest from the equator are the coldest. Temperate regions fall between these extremes.

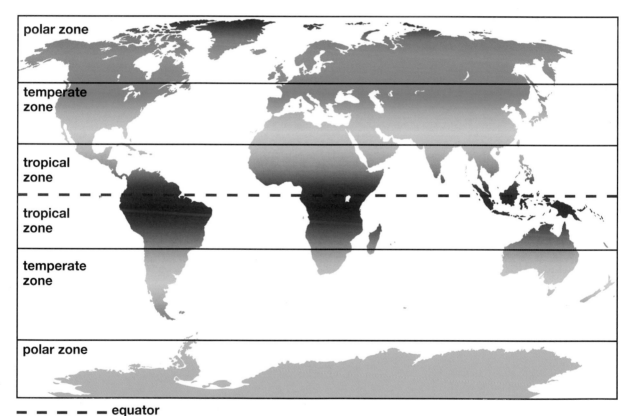

polar zone

temperate zone

tropical zone

tropical zone

temperate zone

polar zone

– – – – – equator

But latitude is just one piece of the climate puzzle. The desert climate in Death Valley, California, for example, differs greatly from the milder climate just a couple hundred miles away in Los Angeles. That's because Los Angeles sits along the coast of the Pacific Ocean. A region's location on the continent and its distance from other bodies of water makes a difference.

Death Valley in the Mojave Desert is the hottest, driest, lowest place in the United States, sitting at 282 feet (86 meters) below sea level. Average yearly rainfall is 2.36 inches (6 centimeters), and the hottest temperature ever recorded there was 134°F (57.1°C) on July 10, 1913.

Types of Climate Regions

The most common way to categorize climate types comes from a scientist named Wladimir Köppen (1846-1940). He recognized that different types of plants grow in different regions depending on the climate. He proposed five major climate types in 1900. Each region also has climate subtypes.

Tropical climates have high temperatures throughout the year. They include wet rainforests and monsoon climates, which have a wet season and a dry season. By contrast, dry climates get very little rain year-round. They include the desert and have big swings in temperature from day to night.

Moderate climates have seasons with mild winters and can be humid and rainy or dry. Continental climates fall between moderate climates and polar climates. They have the most variation in seasons with warm summers and cold, snowy winters. Polar regions include the tundra and ice caps at the North and South poles.

The oceans have a major effect on regional and worldwide climates because they cover 70 percent of the Earth's surface. Ocean currents and wind currents affect the water cycle and move the sun's energy from the equator to the rest of the world.

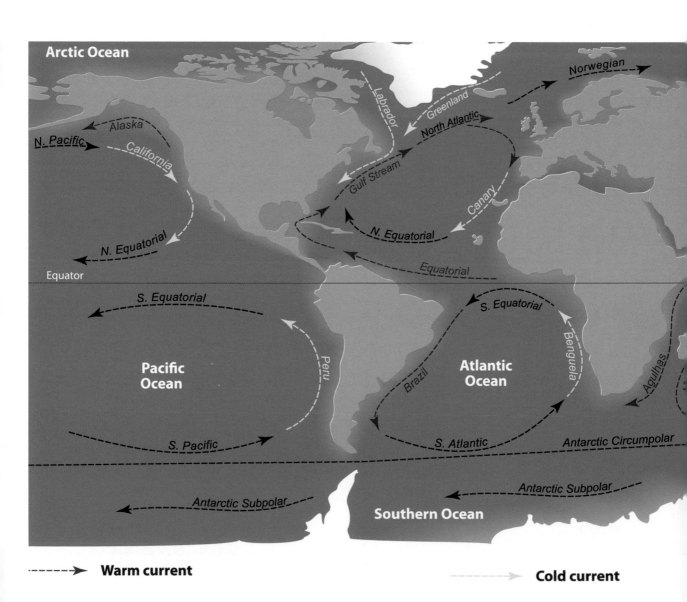

The terrain and elevation of an area affect its climate too. Even though the equator passes through Ecuador, only about half of that country has a tropical climate. The high elevation of the Andes Mountains in Ecuador creates much colder climates in these areas.

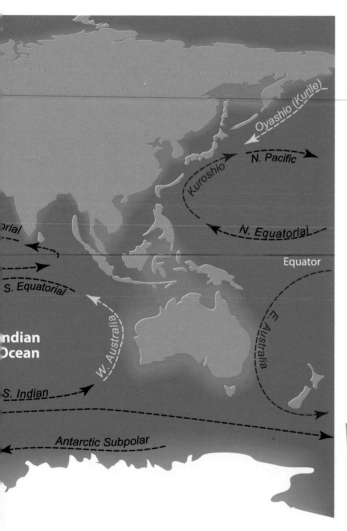

Neutral current

Mount Kilimanjaro

Most areas have only one climate, but when you climb Mount Kilimanjaro, Africa's tallest mountain, you pass through five different climate zones. The mountain's base is surrounded by farmland that gives way to rainforest as you climb to the first 9,000 feet (2,800 meters). Next you enter heather and moorland, with sparser plants, short shrubs, and mossy trees. Around 13,000 feet (4,000 meters), you enter the brown, dry alpine desert, with warm days and freezing nights. The last zone is the snowy, almost lifeless Arctic zone, from about 16,500 feet (5,000 meters) to the summit at 19,341 feet (5,895 meters).

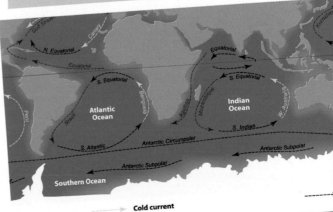

Cold current

Climate Change

Over time, climate changes. During extremely cold periods in the Earth's history, much of today's land was covered with glaciers and ice sheets. Then, as the Earth warmed up, the ice would melt and cause flooding. Animals and plants had to adapt to these changes in climate.

Human Activity and Climate Change

The most significant way people cause climate change is by increasing the concentration of greenhouse gases in the atmosphere. These gases absorb the sun's heat and keep the planet warm. They include carbon dioxide, methane, and nitrous oxide. When the atmosphere has too much of them, the Earth gradually heats up.

Burning fossil fuels, such as oil, coal, and natural gas, increases the carbon dioxide in the atmosphere. Raising animals for meat increases the methane released, and clearing forests from the land reduces the number of trees, which take carbon dioxide out of the atmosphere and turn it into oxygen.

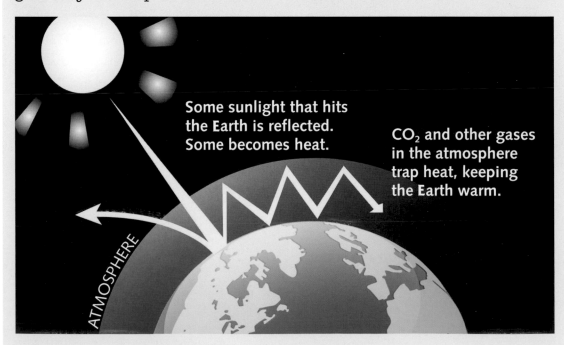

Some sunlight that hits the Earth is reflected. Some becomes heat.

CO_2 and other gases in the atmosphere trap heat, keeping the Earth warm.

ATMOSPHERE

Scientists learn about past climates by studying tree rings, layers of sediment in the ground, and samples of ice frozen for many years. They have learned several natural factors can cause climate change. Over the past million years, slight changes in the Earth's orbit and tilt caused ice sheets to grow and shrink on 100,000–year cycles. Over millions of years, movements of the Earth's tectonic plates and changes in the sun's energy have affected ocean currents and changed the climate. Large volcanic eruptions can also change global weather for a few years.

The 2010 eruption of Iceland's Eyjafjallajökull volcano spewed ash into the atmosphere that lasted for several months.

Each ring of a tree represents a year and will have a different thickness and other features depending on the atmospheric conditions that year.

People also contribute to changes in the climate. In fact, the climate is warming up faster now than it has in the past 10,000 years. The average temperature across the world went up about 1.8 degrees Fahrenheit (1 degree Celsius) during the 20th century. Most scientists believe human activities play the biggest role in this warming and that global temperature will continue rising at a faster rate. That means only people can make changes to slow it down.

Boulder Glacier in Glacier National Park, Montana 1910

Boulder Glacier in Glacier National Park, Montana 2007

What Climate Change Means

Global warming can create many challenges. As polar ice caps melt, sea levels rise. Higher sea levels will put some coastal communities in danger of higher flooding or lost beach land. The temperature increase also influences precipitation, crops, water supplies, human health, and the functioning of ecosystems. Scientists expect more severe weather, such as heat waves, droughts, and floods, with the increase. Plants and animals will have to adapt to the changes to survive, and many species will probably go extinct.

Slowing down or reversing these climate changes will require coordination from people and countries across the world. Individuals can play a small role by recycling materials, using less water and electricity, and driving less. Leaders across the world are trying to work together to find ways to slow down global warming.

Some people live close enough to work to commute by bicycle instead of by car. Bicycle commuting means less oil use and less carbon dioxide released into the atmosphere.

45

Glossary

air pressure (air PRESH-ur): the density or weight of the air, which is greater near the Earth than it is high up

atmosphere (AT-muhs-feer): the mixture of gases that surrounds a planet

condensation (kahn-den-SAY-shuhn): the changing of a gas or vapor into its liquid form

convection (kuhn-VEK-shuhn): the circulation of heat through liquids and gases

equator (i-KWAY-tur): an imaginary line around the middle of the Earth that is an equal distance from the North and South Poles

gravity (GRAV-i-tee): the force that pulls things toward the center of the Earth and keeps them from floating away

hemisphere (HEM-i-sfeer): one half of a round object, especially of the Earth

humidity (hyoo-MID-i-tee): the amount of moisture in the air

meteorology (mee-tee-uh-RAH-luh-jee): the study of Earth's atmosphere, especially in relation to climate and weather

momentum (moh-MEN-tuhm): force or speed that something gains when it is moving

precipitation (pri-sip-i-TAY-shuhn): the falling of water from the sky in the form of rain, sleet, hail, or snow

radiation (ray-dee-AY-shuhn): the giving off of energy in the form of light or heat

satellites (SAT-uh-lites): spacecraft that is sent into orbit around the Earth, the moon, or another heavenly body

temperature (TEM-pur-uh-chur): the degree of heat or cold in something, usually measured by a thermometer

tides (tides): the constant change in sea level that is caused by the pull of the sun and the moon on the Earth

Index

Show What You Know

1. How do the Earth and sun together cause the seasons?
2. What causes the wind?
3. How do scientists predict the weather?
4. What's the difference between weather and climate?
5. What's causing climate change and what can humans do about it?

Websites to Visit

pmm.nasa.gov/education/
www.noaa.gov/
virtualskies.arc.nasa.gov/weather/index.html

About the Author

Tara Haelle spent much of her youth exploring creeks and forests outside and reading books inside. Her adventures got bigger when she became an adult and began traveling across the world to go on exciting adventures such as swimming with sharks, climbing Mt. Kilimanjaro, and exploring the Amazon. She earned a photojournalism degree from the University of Texas at Austin so she could keep learning about the world by interviewing scientists and writing about their work. She currently lives in central Illinois with her husband and two sons. You can learn more about her at her website: www.tarahaelle.net.

Meet The Author!
www.meetREMauthors.com

www.rourkeeducationalmedia.com

PHOTO CREDITS: Cover: Fall Trees© Botond Horvath, background clouds © MidoSemsem, moons © oriontrail, Earth © MarcelClemens; page 4 © Alessandro Colle, page 5 © Naskies; page 6 © Milagli; page 7 © Mike Vande Ven Jr; page 8 © pockygallery, page 9 © BlueRingMedia; page 10-11 © Lenka_X, page 11 © BlueRingMedia, page 12-13 © © Somchai Som , page 12 inset © S.Borisov; page 14 © Designua, page 15 bottom © Anders Persson; page 16 © Andy Cash, page 16-17 © Francesco Carucci; page 18-19 © Valery Bareta, page 18 inset © peresanz, page 19 © noaa; page 20-21 © jakelv7500, page 22 © Artur Synenko; page 24 © Andrey Armyagov, page 25 both photos © noaa; page 26-27 © valdezrl, page 27 cold front diagram © Designua; page 28 inset © Christian Bertrand, page 28-29 © Circumnavigation, page 30-31 © FashionStock.com, page 31 © Narongsak Nagadhana; page 32 © Harvepino, page 33 © Dave Weaver; page 34 © solarseven, page 35 © Dan Craggs; page 36 © ventdusud, page 37 © Smit; page 38 © Dmstudio | Dreamstime.com, page 39 © Vezzani Photography; page 40 map © Designua, page 41 © Andrzej Kubik; page 43 volcano © K.Narloch-Liberra, tree rings © Sergieiev; page 44 top © courtesy GNP Archives, bottom © Blase Reardon (USGS), page 45 cyclists © connel, recycling bins © gnohz

Edited by: Keli Sipperley

Cover and Interior design by: Nicola Stratford   www.nicolastratford.com

Library of Congress PCN Data

Seasons, Tides, and Lunar Phases / Tara Haelle
(Let's Explore Science)
 ISBN 978-1-68191-395-7 (hard cover)
 ISBN 978-1-68191-437-4 (soft cover)
 ISBN 978-1-68191-476-3 (e-Book)
Library of Congress Control Number: 2015951562

Also Available as:
ROURKE'S
e-Books

Printed in the United States of America, North Mankato, Minnesota